WORK IS LOVE
MADE VISIBLE

The Little Family, after apple picking.
Kingston, Oklahoma, ca. 1920

WORK IS LOVE MADE VISIBLE

Poems

and Family Photographs

Jeanetta Calhoun Mish

West End Press

Albuquerque, New Mexico
2009

Some of these poems have previously appeared in the following periodicals, journals, and collections: *LABOR: Studies in Working-Class History of the Americas*; *Tongue Tied Woman* (winner, 2001 Edda/Soulspeak Poetry Chapbook Competition for Women); *WLT2*; *Poetry Bay*; *Oklahoma Today*; and *The Long Islander*. Poems have also been published in two anthologies: *Returning the Gift* and *The Colour of Resistance*.

Special thanks to the IAO poetry group and Woody Guthrie Poets, Nathan Brown, Phil Morgan, and Norbert Krapf for support and assistance. Gratitude for last-minute inspiration to the Blue Moon on Paseo and the western swing band The Townies. And a high five to Charlie Mish for keeping me cool.

Work Is Love Made Visible is the third publication in the West End Press
New Series, featuring full-length volumes by emerging
and recently recognized poets.

Printed in the United States of America.
First printing: March 2009

ISBN 978-0-9816693-3-5

Typography and book design by Bryce Milligan.
Cover photo from family archives of the author (see notes).
Inside author photo by Charles Patrick Mish.

West End Press
P.O. Box 27334
Albuquerque, NM 87125

This book is dedicated to my husband,
Kyran Daniel John Mish.

He actually deserves medals for his
courage, consistency, compassion, constancy, and competence,
but I hope this book will suffice.

All work is empty save when there is love . . .
Work is love made visible.

– Kahlil Gibran

Contents

Rosasharn Reports

Rosasharn Reports from California in the 21st Century   3
Seekers   5
Road Bums   6
Dysfunction in Three Movements   7
Roughneck's Love Song   8
collateral damage   9
For the People of New Orleans   10
two art lessons   11
What I See   12
program of worship: mount shasta wilderness sanctuary   13
midwinter   15

Home Oklahoma

suite: home oklahoma   18
ashes and dust   19
Storyteller   20
The Etymology of Honky Tonk   22
after working tomato plants with my mother   24
For Michael   25
Body Snatcher   27
Remnants   29
for my brother   30
My Great Great Grandmother Writes the Perfect Poem   35
My Sister's Sacrifice   37
Work Is Love Made Visible   40
A Woman's Inheritance   42
Grandpa's Bouquet   46
Lessons from Luke   49

Mapping Desire

mapping desire   52
the music, the boys   53
Promises   54

Conviction   55
Morning Star   56
Falling Stars   57
On the Death of Your Cat, Jack Kerouac   58
To Ask and Be Answered   60

Notes on the Photographs   62
About the Author   64

ROSASHARN REPORTS

The poet's great-grandmother, and in the doorway, her grandfather. Odell, Marshall County, Oklahoma, ca. 1918.

Rosasharn Reports from California
in the 21st Century

The first thing I need to tell you-all
is that I am not the same girl
you saw last in that book of Mr. Steinbeck's
Times have changed and so have I.

I've been taking classes at the open campus in Davis—
literature classes, since I figured I knew
a little something about literature.
But all those other students want to talk about
is that near to last scene that they say
is full of madonna symbolism.
You know the one I mean.

And the teacher pointed out to me how
Tom is the Christ-figure and how I am the virgin-figure.
I was a bit discomfited by them talking that way
but they assured me it was all about symbolism
and not about religion.
They talk too about the virgin-whore dichotomy
but I tole them right quick I wasn't no whore
Anyway, they say I'm quite the character
even though Mr. Steinbeck's "virile, realist style"
is "no longer viable." Wouldn't you just know it?
Plain talk is out of fashion.

Well, while I'm spoutin' off about plain talk
I best be doin' some of my own.
To tell it to you straight,
I ain't changed that much
and neither have the times.

I been travelin' up and down the central valley
and I wrote out a postcard that said
"having a great time, wish you were here"
but I tore it up 'cause I wasn't quite sure it tole the truth.
Most the white folks livin' in the valley are Okies,
two or three generations removed.
But they seem to have forgot where they came from;
they're all a-votin' republican
and supportin' strike-breakers and refusing a
helpin' hand to those Mexicans working
in the same fields their grandparents hoed.

Tomorrow I'm headin' over to San Francisco.
I hear the folks there are concerned about the workers
and about the pollution that's kicked up by all these cars.
They got programs to help out the poor kids
and programs to help out the sick people
and programs to make the neighborhoods pretty.

I met some fine people from there so
don't put too much stock in what you hear.
It's true that some of them are funny, well, you know what I mean . . .
but the only thing different about them is who they love
and right now, sittin' here in Stockton
watchin' whole families sleep in the park,
I figure we could use a lot more love and a lot more programs
and lot less hate and intolerability.

Oh, yeah, there's one more thing I meant to tell ya:
those folks from San Francisco—they ast me if I knew Woody.
It was nice to be remembered of somebody from home.

Seekers

All afternoon I have sensed the gathering tempest—
the smothering humidity, the still air,
prophetic clouds and dry lightning,
thunder spreading across the plains.
I go outside to watch the storm,
to inhale ozone into my deepest alveoli
as if it were some kind of magic elixir.
My neighbors, too, stand with their heads back,
contemplating the sky, interpreting signs and portents;
the wind becomes our prayer, the rain our baptism.
Our anxious worship is interrupted by the
trumpet-blast of a tornado warning on channel 4.
A moment later, a fierce wind arrives and
drives us away from whatever it is we sought
in the roiling black clouds on the western horizon.

Road Bums

for Sharon Doubiago

On my way to a home to a town I no longer recognize,
I'll spend twenty-six hours in the back of the bus;
just now, fifteen hours out from New York City
and Terre Haute is rising from the plains of Indiana.

Bus conversation is governed by a set of rules
instinctively understood—long silences interrupted
by bursts of conversation about nothing and everything.
When the silence comes I write in my journal
and try to remember if I've ever read a road bum poem by a woman.

It's as if we never go anywhere alone
but here I am and there is the gray-haired lady
sitting beside me who just got her college degree at age sixty
and in front of us, a pale thin girl who can't be more than sixteen
but whose tattoos insist she has lots of mileage.
The three of us manage sporadic revelations
about our lives and the no-good men we've known.
The Chicana behind us never says anything;
she hums *corridos* to herself and cries.
Across the aisle, Lateesha spends most of her time reading the Bible,
but she shares her last piece of chocolate with me.

Invisibility is an asset when women travel alone
and perhaps our freedom is too precious for words,
so precious we avoid the inevitable domestications and interpretations,
instead, keep this to ourselves:

> this company of wild women
> laughing and crying, drinking and smoking
> praying and swearing, independent and raucous

in the back of the bus

Dysfunction in Three Movements

1.
A child's shoe is stuck in a red clay embankment alongside
 historic route 66,
two tiny lacy white socks are nailed to a tree;
further down the road, a pink stuffed bear.

2.
A song about welfare mothers booms from the speakers in
 my truck.
On Reno Boulevard I see a sad-eyed woman alight from a
 black BMW;
her pvc dress and cheap patent boots reflect the red
neon "Goodwill to Men" sign flashing above Bill's
 Low-Cost Liquor.

A bitter wind toys with her scarf.
Her hollow eyes proposition every passing car;
her sagging belly tells of recent expectations.

Maybe if i tell her Neil Young wrote a song for her
it would fill one of those blank spaces in her eyes.

3.
It is Sunday, July 4 at 10:30 pm
in an all-night grocery in Joplin Missouri.
Two women shuffle up to the express lane
cradling gallon whiskey jugs and
two-liter bottles of seven-up.
Their hungry dirty children cling to mama's legs
crying and begging for food,

celebrating independence day.

Roughneck's Love Song

I left her, you know
right there in dust blown
West Texas.

Helluva gal. I mean, I'm not
sure what took me over.

Just one mornin'
I woke up and she
didn't look like any
body I knew

so I lit out.

collateral damage

imagine. refugees huddling
waiting for warmth to throw back the shadows
the mountains moving imperceptibly toward dawn

look. a small boy is picking up a stone, but it
is a stone made for throwing, not for skipping
he has forgotten how to play
he hurls the stone toward hidden enemies
and wipes away the water in his eye

see. this young woman should be
blossoming but hunger and fatigue have
nipped her budding
she is dirty, her feet blistered from
the miles between bombs and borders
who will light a candle for her
if she withers here in this bare soil

here in the devastated city,
the flower vendor has left the street corner
having no one to lean on, the fresh flowers sign
is swaying madly in the wind

For the People of New Orleans

Because I have seen visions of the apocalypse on cable tv
my poems have taken a turn to the biblical.
It is not the natural disaster I cannot comprehend;
we live and we die by nature's hand.

The man-made catastrophe is what stuns me:
thousands of abject human beings trapped
in the civic center and the superdome,
hunched under the eaves of their inundated homes
days after the hurricane passed.

How can we ever explain to ourselves and to our children
the unanswered chant of "help, help, help, help"
echoing through drowned New Orleans for six days
long enough, it is said, to create heaven and earth.

two art lessons

1. composition
at six am
a pink and purple sunrise
washes through plate glass windows on the third floor
i shade my eyes while hunting for a fresh vein
just below the shirtsleeve tanline of a man
whose chest is freshly scored by the knife
sparks of sunlight glint off the staples on his sternum
in this sterile suite, surrounded by severe machines
he lies silent and ashen-faced on stiff white sheets
stunned, alive

2. perspective
on my third trip to the emergency room tonight
i have come to pierce an artery
my target is an old woman
whose left breast has been gouged away
with no thought of aesthetics
her mouth is twisted with paralysis
yet she struggles to speak
she wants me to know how concerned she is
for the little girl in the next bed

What I See

Walking across campus
I see a woman from landscaping
pulling in a hundred foot, one inch hose;
her strong arms and knotty shoulders
glistening with sweat.
I say "Who needs the gym?"
She laughs, replies "No shit!"

Thirty feet above me on his scaffold I see
a master bricklayer load a trowel with mortar
then apply it with polished full-arm sweep
finished in a delicate twist of his wrist.
An intricate pattern emerges on the building's facade.
"Beautiful work," I call and he answers
with a smile and a cavalier's bow.

I see James coming down the hall
bouncing his push broom along,
pop pop shush, pop pop shush
"Didja go fishin' this weekend?" I ask.
He stops, smiles a devilish grin,
then snaps his broom up horizontally across his chest
declares, "I got one this big."

I see a young student who specializes in theory
and agitates for the graduate assistants' union,
but he doesn't see James and his mighty fish.
He bumps into James from behind, then goes on,
never looking up from Postmodern Marxisms,
muttering to himself about his upcoming presentation
on the fusion between theory and practice.

program of worship:
mount shasta wilderness sanctuary

here on the mountain where
mind and body and spirit work together
where sweat is as valid a sacrifice as
coins of the realm tossed into a brass bowl,
i don my ceremonial garb:
olive drab ripstop shorts with six pockets
and an orange t-shirt from moab
lace my hiking boots tight at the ankle
easier over the instep,
cover my head with "life is good" cap,

i pull on the backpack, fill the hydrator.
then pause by small kiosk at trailhead to register my visit,
and take up the proffered stewardship container

gazing skyward, i scan for small metal trail markers
nailed into trees above snowline.
taking moment of silence, i contemplate the reckoning
that snowline is at least twenty feet above my head
and remember that the soaring arches of cathedrals
were designed to imitate the heavens

i place my foot firmly on the well-worn trail
and adjust my body's angle to the slope
my bended knee genuflects toward a white lupine
my meditation centers on all creation
i take my first step. all journeys begin this way.

my song of praise tunes itself to the wind organ
piping along the black edge where basalt meets blue sky
a child's laughter sounds a trumpet
the wind in the pines is the bone whistle's call

my footsteps in scree are a turtle shell rattle,
my heart the deepest drum.

i obey the mother eagle's scolding for silence
just as i did granny's deft pinch and stern look
when i wiggled and thumped too much
on wooden pews when a child

i listen for the silence inside sound
and enter the wisdom of Be Still and Know
suddenly things divided become whole again.

i fall to my knees in a stand of coyote mint
and place a leaf on my tongue, a pungent host.
i remember the center of the universe is within
and repeat the phrase as an apostles' creed.

arriving at the end of the trail, i look up,
because for all time, petitioners have always looked up.

i look up toward the sacred summit and pray.

midwinter

yellow apples turning
wrinkly brown in the bowl invite
visions of august's persimmons
frostbitten mahogany orbs
ripening near the chicken coop
at grandpa's farm

summer demands so much of us
the glare, the heat, the danger
midwinter settles in
like a familiar hand
on the back of the neck

the early darkness bids us consider
that the way we recognize
the sweetness of comfort
is that our tongues remember
the bitterness of sorrow

HOME
OKLAHOMA

suite: home oklahoma

I. canadian river bottom

a ribbon of early morning light
rests softly on a backbone ridge in the distance
my shoes are stained with red clay

the rain crow calls, and if i listen closely
i can hear inside his lonely voice a dim memory
i ask him to show me the way home

II. wewoka

i remember being startled by seeing my brown face
reflected in the dimestore window
superimposed on packages of bed linen
marked down for the white sale

III. at the stompdance grounds

for cynthia johnson

we sit in the arbor on a cool misty evening
a red flower dances in a shimmering water glass
the sun's glare has softened,
its rays round themselves on the horizon,
reaching across the sky to illuminate
the shiniest thread of a spider's web
suspended in time above the table

ashes and dust

it has taken my garden to remind me
how intimately life lies with death
the gold sacks of bone meal and blood meal
the shocking charnel house stink of hydrated lime
every square foot of loamy soil amended by decay
yet for five generations my family's strong hands
have crumbled red dirt clods, sown precious seeds
and pulled weeds until our fingers ached
our palms callous to match the rake and hoe
we invest ourselves in the bones and the blood
and wring life from the ashes and dust

Storyteller

for Louisa Ellen Exendine Sanderson

I drive toward the arms of the Canadian river,
it calls to me, jealous of the Hudson
murmuring beneath my window
through long winter nights.

In Oklahoma an owl waits silently
amid the rubble of my grandmother's house.
Her face shines out from its eyes,
its wings brush the cracked edges of memory.

The tires hum, an intermittent rain sequins the windshield,
a shy moon hides behind a veil of black clouds.
Radio stations fade in and out with the passing miles
and an urgent wind impels me westward.

Grandmother
you were silenced before you could
begin to tell me the stories;
I am coming home.
I am listening everywhere
for your voice.

Left to right: the poet's great-great grandmother Louisa Ellen Exendine Sanderson, and her great-grandmother, Gertrue Iness Little Sanderson, ca. 1925.

The Etymology of Honky Tonk

for Nathan Brown

Its dancing seeds arrived in Oklahoma Territory
along with those of red wheat and tumbleweed
hidden in the pockets of Russian-German immigrants.
It was cultivated with a fiddle bow grasped
in the calloused hand of a Scots-Irish farmer
and given the blues by Freedmen
singing in black township roadhouses.
Its rhythm was established by a defiant Indian drum
echoing down a river valley in the spring.
Someone's little brother gave it words and
simple chords strummed on a mail-order guitar;
at the age of thirty it got some swing and
learned syncopatin' from a Count and a Duke.
Its lonesome cry slid in from Hawaii
twelve strings and two pedals on a hurricane wind.
Just yesterday it was crooning to a blue moon
and flirting with a saxophone player.

It is a sound and a song and a sanctuary;
it is a place and a plea and a prayer
and it calls you out to sit in with the band
because it knows you remember the tune.

The first documented print usage of the term "honk-a-tonk" is found in The
Daily Ardmorite *(Oklahoma), February 26, 1894.*

The poet's grandparents, great-grandparents, and great-aunts
and uncles. Sky View Club, Duncan, Oklahoma, ca. 1951.

after working tomato plants with my mother

my mother has planted tomatoes in her flower garden and
they have run amok, their viney arms smothering the
petunias and snapping the lithe waist of the day lily. it is an
odd compunction, this familial urge to plant tomatoes even
in the smallest block tiled patio; i have felt the urge myself
and wondered what kind of tomatoes would bear their juicy
red fruits in western new york or in colorado at 10,000 feet
in the rocky mountains, maybe staked in a terracotta pot
intended for ivy or some other more civilized, less elemental
growth. we untangle thumb thick vines and prune away dead
stems and lengths that do not bear even one tiny yellow
blossom. tomato plant smell is everywhere, its bitter odor
and our laughter floating on a small hot wind that has arisen
from somewhere in a hollow on the great plains.

For Michael

Listen:
one day when you were three,
in the time of living in the mountains
in the time of waterfalls and rainbows
hummingbird was lost—
trapped inside a window,
crumpled in the corner of the sill,
his body heaving.

I scooped him up with my mommy hands—
the hands you gave me to hold you when you cried.
You caressed his feathers shimmering
iridescent in the late afternoon light;
outside, under a trembling aspen
I raised my arms, opened my hands and
hummingbird flew toward the sun.

I want to tell you this story
so you know that the most unlikely hours
hold manifest blessings.
I want you to know
I have learned to let go.

The poet's mother and brother. Seminole, Oklahoma, 1979.

Body Snatcher

for my mother

1.
This fall instead of wearing jeans,
I scoured garage sales and thrift stores
for wool tweed and corduroy trousers
bought new bras for the first time in years
pushed my scraggly hair back under a head band
and found a nice brown shade of lipstick that didn't have a
    life of its own.
I can't exactly explain why except that
I outgrew all my jeans and thought it was time for a change.

2.
I walked by the mirror yesterday and gasped in recognition.
When did your face grow onto mine?
I imagine myself a Body Snatcher,
slowly forming into you in black and white hysteria,
each new line and gray hair sucking a moment of life out
    of the original.
I am both pleased and frightened by the transformation.
You are still so beautiful yet who will I be if I become you?
I fought so long and so hard to avoid this inevitability.

When I was a child
there were two photographs I always confused,
one is black and white the other color, but otherwise
they seem to be of the same dark-haired big-eyed dreamer child.

Tell me again, momma
which one was me and which you?

3.
A mass
you reported they said;
not a bump or a polyp or something less sinister.
I wonder, does the tumor grow upon the moment
the police called to say that I had overdosed on crank
or perhaps the mass was seeded in the year
I didn't call or visit but instead wrote to your mother
complaining that you just didn't understand my lifestyle.

You said the doctors would know next week
but I will never know for sure.

4.
Maurice wrote an entire book of poems about his mother
but for you, the truth-telling required would be
an invasion of privacy—a hanging out of dirty laundry—
so I won't write that book just now
but instead I give you this one poem,
the best prayer I have to offer.

Remnants

At eight-thirty on Thursday mornings
Mrs. Cohen would roll deep canvas bins
out onto the breezeway in front of her dry goods store.
Those bins brimmed with exotic treasures:
remnants of velvet, bolt ends of silk,
ruby red polished cotton and stern grey wool.

My mother and I were always among the first to
dive into that sea of possibilities.
This print here would make a nice shirt for sister.
This deep green chenille—bathrobes for Christmas gifts.

By nine o'clock, twenty women stooped over the bins,
laughing and talking, consoling and condoling,
gossiping and shushing, exchanging knowing looks
and arched eyebrows above their daughters' heads.

By nine-thirty, the bins would be empty,
the week's news disseminated, the judgments made.
The scraps and pieces of our small town
bundled and tied, taken home to be cut to pattern
and sewn into something respectable.

for my brother

1. what I wrote

Phillip Wayne Inman passed away Friday night in his home
in Lewisville, Texas. He was 47 years old. Phillip was born in
Wewoka, Oklahoma, November 17, 1957, and he graduated
from Wewoka High School in 1976. Phillip joined the Army
National Guard with the 45th Infantry Division in 1977. He
later joined the United States Army and served honorably
for sixteen years in the 7th, 37th, and 18th Field Artilleries.
Phillip received commendations for his service in Operation
Safe Haven in the Republic of Panama and numerous
other commendations, including two Army Commendation
Medals. Since leaving the Army, Phillip had worked as a
long haul truck driver and as a crane operator. He will always
be remembered for his ready smile and his ability to put in
a long day's hard work with pride. Former SSG Inman will
have graveside services with military honors.

The poet's brother, Phillip, 1996.

2. what I didn't write

truth is my brother's life never really got started. berated,
beaten, broken by our stepfather. escaped to the sanctuary
of our grandparents home bewildered and betrayed. in high
school he took a vo-tech certificate in diesel mechanics but
couldn't find a job. so soldier it was and he was good at it,
the books full of commendations and those military
college hours he thought would help him when he looked
into going to college later but funding for GI bill went down
and all those hours meant nothing to the university, he'd
have to start over. but anyway back in the army his childhood
terrors chased him around and into the bottle and the army
sent him to rehab once twice three times then said we'll give
you an honorable if you'll go quietly four years before you're
eligible for retirement. same with the truck driving jobs, the
stockroom jobs the janitor jobs but not with the crane
operator job he was sober his life was looking up. it paid well
but he hadn't been there long enough for insurance when he
had the stroke at 43 and of course it was not an on the job
injury and it took too long to get well and he would've been
a safety risk so if he'd go quietly they'd say he was laid off
so he could collect unemployment. then he found out from
the v.a. doctor after months of waiting that he'd had the
stroke because he had a bad heart and the doc said here's the
prescription you need but the v.a. doesn't approve that drug
so brother went without. and had been going without for
some time when his landlord, angry about late rent went up
to my brother's apartment and the smell overcame him and
he called the police and my brother left in a body bag after
eight days there on the floor dropped dead doing laundry.
every article of clothing folded with sharp corners every
surface in the house spotless, the bed made, the pillows
fluffed. eight days because he was between jobs and had
moved for the tenth time to a cheaper place and knew
nobody. eight days worth of unheard messages on the

answering machine, some about being hired in the warehouse of a famous big box store three messages then no more. eight days because he was one day overdue to see his mom and granny but they usually didn't worry about just twenty-four hours overdue because phillip wayne was that way. momma said, sister, you're good at writing would you write another obituary first grandpa's then dad's now brother's would you write it we can't trust it to the funeral home or the newspaper and i said yes because that's what i do i wrote it but what i really wanted to do was curse. curse the violent stepfather curse the meanness of a small town curse the men who beat my mother curse the lack of work curse the joke of a healthcare system in this country curse myself for not knowing he hadn't been well for not knowing he had lain there alone for so long. i wrote then as i'm writing now when what i really want to do is cry. O Bubba. O Phip. who now to tell me "aw, hell, sis—we've been through worse and lived."

The poet's great-great-grandmother at the Busy Bee Cafe, ca. 1938.

My Great-Great-Grandmother Writes
the Perfect Poem

Mary Ellen stands outside the Busy Bee cafe,
a corrugated metal building
with a hand-painted "Open" sign,
its shabbiness evident in the harsh light.
Her left thumb is hooked over her pocket,
her tiny wire glasses almost invisible in the
photograph taken in Tonopah, Nevada;
it was the late Thirties and the town was dying.
Silver mine dust settled everywhere,
on cafe tables and on window sills
and inside her faded bedroom.

When Mary Ellen was thirty, her husband and two
sons died, poisoned with some unknown substance
while camped in a lovely clearing at the side of the road.
Found with their faces blue and their coffee cups half empty,
the banked coals still warm from the night before.
When she recovered, she remarried and
her new husband took her out to Tonopah;
maybe her bruised heart found a home in the desert
that sparse land with no trees and few rivers
so different from lush north Texas.

She wrote poetry there, at a red-checked oilcloth-
covered table in the Busy Bee cafe, whenever
she wasn't serving the dwindling stream of customers
or bussing worn-out tables or washing chipped dishes.
She mailed her poems to the Christian Science Monitor
and they published more than one, delicate
intricate victorian verse, rhymed and metered.

But I believe her perfect poem is written
on the back of the Busy Bee photograph, where,
despite the sorrows of her life and the rusting facade,
she wrote: *this is where I feed the hungry.*

My Sister's Sacrifice

In most of her pictures
my sister is standing by the door
because she's always leaving.
Sometimes she doesn't come back for a while
a short while or a long one and
we're never sure where she goes.
My mother worries and grieves
my granny comforts my mother
and everyone thinks I don't care
because we never got along too well.

There are sightings,
as if she were a u.f.o.
She's been caught in Killeen,
married to a soldier,
found in Granger Falls,
waitressing at Denny's,
spotted in Odessa,
dancing at the Wild Cherry.
But mostly she returns
to where we grew up,
a mean withered blight of a town
where she can hide
in the homes of friends
who I never knew and
my mother finds trashy.

To appreciate my sister's sacrifice
it is necessary to understand
that *where* she goes is not the question;

the question is *why* she goes
and despite appearances to the contrary
I care why she goes because she goes in my stead.

She goes away to refute our circumstances.
She goes away to battle our past.
She goes away because we both know
that it is futile to lock the door at night
when the boogieman is inside;
that there is no reason to stay home
when home is the last place you want to go.

The poet's sister, 1982.

Work Is Love Made Visible

After working all day, at home or at the garment factory
or taking care of her mother or her grandchildren,
after cooking dinner and cleaning up the kitchen
my granny would uncover her sewing machine
and stitch our family together.

Her love for me is a green paisley dress with a matching purse
constructed when I was eight and tucked into bed in the
    next room,
the sewing machine humming into my dreams.
Her love for me is a 1970s high fashion three-piece suit:
bellbottom pants, vest, blazer with broad lapels
made of faux suede patchwork in orange and brown.

Even now, I can recite every article of granny's handiwork,
proclaim the delight of something made just for me,
sing the alchemy of love and labor,
testify that after working all day, day after day,
my granny would sit at her sewing machine
and attire me in vestments of love.

The poet's grandmother. Chickasha, Oklahoma, ca 1940.

A Woman's Inheritance

My great grandma Bessie went to business school and learned how
to put her property in her own name, even in Texas,
so she could leave it to her daughters instead her husband.
She had a fine and analytical mind;
she taught me to always ask questions,
especially when I wasn't supposed to.

Bessie had three sisters, Pearl, Mildred, and Ruth.
Aunt Ruth was a tall willowy woman with a regal carriage.
In the Thirties she worked as a shoe model for a year;
she had impeccable style, which I don't but I do like shoes.
Aunt Pearl was an artist who painted a lushly conceived still-life
of wisteria branches in bloom that hangs above my desk—
delicate, pendulous purple blossoms rising out of round bronze pot.
Aunt Mildred ran off with a questionable man for love and
    adventure.
Between the four of them there's enough artistic temperament
to keep me teetering always on the edge of reality.

My great grandma Bessie had three daughters,
my granny Jeanette, my aunts Polly and Gloria.
Gloria sings like an angel and her skin is perfect even in old age.
Aunt Polly won the war riveting with hundreds of other Rosies.
In a vintage photo, she vamps in Santa Monica, under the
    Wilshire Motel sign,
her hair tied up in a bandanna, her lovely figure hidden
in bulky dungarees, her left arm lifted in self-representative parody.
Through her I claim my flair for the dramatic.
From my granny I have my name, my temper, and my politics,
and from her father's mother, she of the fantastic name
Addie Malissa Mississippie, I have a gift for growing vegetables.

The poet's great-aunt as Rosie the Riveter.
Santa Monica, California, ca. 1943.

My grandpa's grandma Louisa Ellen was an orphan at twelve,
my father's mother Ola Mae was a child of rape;
the grit in my eye is surely their gift, along with enough Indian
blood that in the summer, strangers greet me in Spanish.
Great granny Iness had eleven children, my grandpa
one of nine who lived long enough to grow up;
she gave me a strong body and a stubborn will.
Her mother, Mary Ella, was less than five foot tall,
but she once knocked her drunken, belligerent husband
upside the head with a cast iron skillet for raising a hand to her.
He quit drinking after that. I want to believe I have her spunk.

But how can I reckon the legacy granted by
Rebecca Last-Name-Unknown in the family tree?
How shall I figure my endowment from the dark, intense woman
in an old family photograph who wears a long wool coat
and cradles in her arms a baby in a christening gown?
Her name and her mother's name are lost to me forever.
A woman's inheritance never marches down time
like our father's names or our brother's birthright;
it is not recoverable from crumbling yellow legal documents.
Their gifts and burdens written on my body, echoing in
    my heart,
make of me a living testament to their unrecorded lives.

A family photo of an unnamed woman.

Grandpa's Bouquet

Late in the evening I sit by your recliner,
your hands, rough from plowing gardens and tending cattle,
caress my little girl hair and soon I'm off to sleep,
crackerjacks, rock candy, and root beer follow me into dream.

At first light you wake me, asking
"Are you going to sleep your life away?"
Granny has bacon and eggs frying in the kitchen;
I wash up and follow the familiar aroma to the table.
It is Saturday, sale day at the stockyards
and you have promised me a new horse;
one splash of Listerine, one of Old Spice and you're ready to go.
You split a piece of Juicy Fruit for the road
half for me, half for you.

I am your shadow,
a strange one among all the boys and men at the sale.
The air in the barn is stained with red dust
thick with the stench of manure and cigarettes and chew.
You bid on horses; I hold my breath
and try to keep my ever-moving hands
out of the sight of the auctioneer.
The copper-penny bay comes home with us.

Back home, you celebrate our success
by slicing open summer in the guise
of the greenest watermelon.
Stabbing a choice piece from its meaty red heart,
you proclaim its virtues.
I bury my face into a crescent;
sweet sticky juice runs down my chin.

Our cows can smell watermelon two acres away;
they line up among the black-eyed susans at the back fence
and jostle for position when we toss them the spent rinds.
Soon, the evening's first lightning bug sends up a tender signal;
crickets and tree frogs take up their place in the choir.

I nuzzle down into your shoulder
inhaling your essence and the odors of the day.

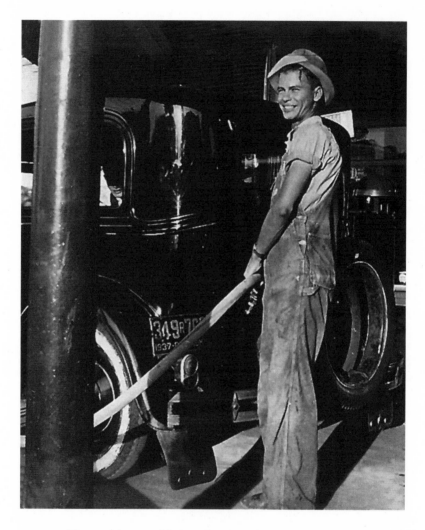

The poet's grandfather, Luther "Luke" Sanderson.
Healdton, Oklahoma, ca. 1937.

Lessons from Luke

Yesterday
I was pruning an overgrown lilac bush
big enough to house three bluebird families
a covey of quail, and one raccoon.
I used the saw-end of a long-handled pruner
to reach the topmost canes
but the results were not equal to the effort.
Then, inside the brusque fall wind I heard
Sister, let the saw do the work.

Last week
I was assembling a new library lamp
to illuminate my beloved collection:
the poems, the novels, the works of philosophy.
I was using a large flat-head screwdriver
to drive a small Phillips-head screw.
The screwdriver slipped and stabbed my hand.
I cursed and in the still moment that followed I heard
Always use the right tool for the job.

This spring
I was preparing ground for my vegetable garden.
It was the hottest spring on record,
it was the end of a painful and difficult time.
The ground was hard and unyielding.
Exhausted and irritated, I walked away
leaving the shovel and hoe lying on the ground.
Suddenly the mockingbird's song had new lyrics:
Take care of your tools and they will take care of you.

Today
I am writing the final draft of an academic paper
and find myself bored with the project,
tired of graduate school and disenchanted with academia,
wondering if I've betrayed myself and my origins,
weary of theories that mean nothing. I want to
skip the last spell-check, write a sloppy conclusion
but the rhythm of the keyboard telegraphs a message:
Any job worth doing is worth doing well.

I answer, OK, Grandpa, and knuckle down.

MAPPING DESIRE

mapping desire

i look like a roadmap, he says,
intending, i suppose, to deflect
any unrealistic expectations of
the power of passing time on
a face i haven't touched in years
but he is forgetting
how i love a road trip
sometimes screaming down the freeway
at 2 am, the bass thumping in the speakers
like the pounding of my heart

most often, though, i like to
take the side roads
roll the windows down
inhale the sweet smells
sheltered under the arching
bowers of trees linked
together like fingers of two hands
spanning what separates them

i like to slide into
a roadhouse on the county line
have a beer, some barbecue and
a slowdance to the blues
then unfold my beloved roadmap
run my finger along a chosen course
imagine all the s-turns and heaves
glory in the forgotten lanes
and remember that the end
of one journey is the
beginning of another

the music, the boys

on any given day it might
be billie testifying about strange fruit
channeled through charlie's strong
fingers taming the steel strings of an
electric guitar or maybe it is the hour
of piano voices like angels because sam
is in the music room mastering randy
newman's cynical god-chords or if the smoky
fog has wrapped around the violin, the longings
of some irish kid with a devilish name come
streaking down the hall and right smack
dab into my heart and sometimes, on nights
when the planets have aligned and the stars rise early
to join the invitation-only audience, their father
sings while they play and there is nothing, nothing
more moving in its harmony, more perfect in its tune

Promises

My mother said it was this way for her:
one morning she would wake up on sheets rougher
than the ones she'd gone to sleep on,
find the coarse hairs in the bathroom sink unexpectedly infuriating—
and she would realize the passion was gone.
She had said I love you and meant it at the time
but the phrase had become a promise
a promise she could not keep.

I lie here awake next to you
your shoulders cast a harsh shadow between us,
your wheezing infuriates me, and I am tired
of climbing out of the swale your body carves.
3 am comes and goes and I wonder
when did it go away, exactly, and
why has it happened, again.
I said I love you and I meant it at the time,
fully aware the phrase becomes a promise.

I thought that just this once
it would be a promise I could keep

Conviction

To the topmost branch of the cedar tree
that has lost most of its limbs to one storm or another
the mockingbird has returned.
He swings with delight on the supple branch
as it bends and sways in the gusty March wind.
He chortles his song and everyone else's
and answers my out-of-tune whistle with glee.
Does he not notice that each year his favorite tree
stands more bare and scarred, that it
weeps great rivers of fragrant resin and groans
and creaks at the slightest spring breeze or
is this his reason for returning, that
the tree could not survive the winter without
the conviction that the mockingbird would return
to sing of regeneration to newly forming branches
and to bring gladness where once there was only despair.

Morning Star

for Norbert

On Long Island
in the quietude of morning
a man rises from his bed,
then tiptoes sock-footed on the stairs,
avoiding the squeaky one halfway down.
He alone is awake,
his son sleeps clutching the violin
that still resonates with
something Russian and passionate;
his wife dreams always of cypress trees
heavy with Spanish moss
and the bayou's pungent hum.

He opens the back door and
pulls on his boots, remembering
his mother who needed him too much,
his father distanced by despair.
He considers his footprints
solitary in the snow
and wonders how it came to be this way,
that poems wake him in the night
and drive him out the door when Venus rules the sky
early, early before first light—
to find redemption in the rhythm of the shovel
and in the blisters on his hands.

Falling Stars

for Kyran

As you climbed into your car to drive to the airport
to gather your son into your arms and into our lives,
the sky chose to celebrate the beginning
of this new adventure by raining down light.
Delighted, you leapt out of the car and ran to the back door near
where I lay in our bed half asleep, chasing a dream of red flowers.

"It's worth it," you said, "to come outside for a while
and watch the Perseids," and because you have never lied to me
I rose and kissed you through the screen
then pulled on one of your old sweatshirts,
went outside, laid on my back and watched the sky.

Stars pirouetted through the heavens
and I thought of the chance we took with each other;
I thought of our children, mine and yours,
I thought of how it would be to grow old with you.

Then I thought again of what you said and
I know that when I draw my last breath
I'll hear your voice again, coming through the window
on a cool August evening and I will reply:

Yes, sweet man.   It was worth it.

On the Death of Your Cat, Jack Kerouac

for Frank Parman

It was a bad year for you
first Ginsberg, then Gogisgi
then Jack Kerouac sliced short by
an anonymous car, right there in
front of the house.

Jack, you said, in a letter that began
"What is it, the moon?" was enthusiastic
about everything, even cars,
liked to luxuriate during a ride around
town swamped in soft upholstery.
His tail long and black and hard
giving you rhythms for your poetry
with its "whomp, whomp" on the floor.

Your friend Ginsberg had his full complement of years,
his passing a reminder of revolutions incomplete.
Gogisgi left too soon, alone and howling in the dark fields
and northern lights of Michigan, without the accolades his
        poetry deserved.
Poor young Jack Kerouac had to be spaded in between
an eye doctor appointment and an argument with an
        inebriated poet.
Jack Kerouac, "He was my friend" you say,
the same goes for Ginsberg and Gogisgi and
that damned drunken poet on the phone.

Do you wonder if you still have enough friends
to fill at least one hand's set of fingers and thumb?

Be careful, be sure to count me—
then leave the gate open for another existentially cool cat
named Allen or Carroll or Claude
to bebop rhythmically whompity whomp through your door.

To Ask and Be Answered

I am thinking of Walt Whitman
because the lilac bush in the backyard is blooming,
because its canes are swaying and rocking,
swaying and rocking in the stiff spring breeze,
because their uncomfortably sweet scent coming
through my bedroom door smells like death,
because I wish I could say *kaddish* for the April deaths
of my grandfather and father and brother,
because an unkindness of ravens has taken up residence
    among the
flowering dead nettles and in their voices
the chant of another whose visions invade my dreams.

I am thinking of Walt Whitman
because I have found myself lonely despite my desires,
because yesterday I wandered in the supermarket
with the ghosts of those two venerable bards and envied their
    eloquence,
because among my intimates I count four poets,
four musicians, and an artist, all thirsty and true,
because I want to embrace my lover but find myself
driving him away with rage and venom,
because I stood a long time last night gazing up
    at the moon and her
beloved Venus
dancing through the moist night-air gathering stars as souvenirs.

I am thinking of Walt Whitman
because there is a certain slant of sorrow in my heart
that has transformed everything;
because I am aching to be expansive,
to embrace the world as it is,

because I believe that loving the world
in its wholeness might save me from melancholy,
because I am convinced that in the refuge of
his wisdom i will find equanimity
because I am desperate for a reaching 'round of his lyrical arms,
desiring to imagine myself sacred in his eyes,
longing to ask and to be answered in affirmation,

are you thinking of me, Walt Whitman?

Notes on the Photographs

Cover Photo: "Ashes and Dust." From left to right: My great-grandmother Iness and her mother, Mary Ella Little. The children: young girl sitting near Mary Ella, my grandfather's older sister, six-year-old Juanita (who died at twelve of scarlet fever); the boy standing in profile with stocking cap is my grandfather, Luther "Luke" Sanderson, age four-and-a-half (Iness had nine more children); the boys are three of Mary Ella's eleven who survived past infancy: her sons, Clyde (with the hoe), Luther Lee, and Sterling (also with a hoe). The family sharecropped the land "on the third" and "on the quarter." Odell, Marshall County, Oklahoma, ca. 1920.

Frontispiece: "The Little Family After Apple Picking." Left to right: Sterling, Ethel, Ellen, Lorena, Grandma Little (Mary Ella), Luther Lee (Bird), Ruth, Iness (the poet's great-grandmother), Grandpa Little (Luther Rice), Maude, Johnny, and Clyde. Kingston, Oklahoma, ca. 1920.

Page 2: Rosasharn would have been at home here with my great-grandmother Iness and three of her eleven surviving children. My grandpa Luther is standing in the doorway. Odell, Marshall County, Oklahoma, ca. 1919.

Page 21: "Storyteller." My great-great-grandmother Louisa Ellen Exendine Sanderson and my great-grandmother Gertrue Iness Little Sanderson. Family lore hints of some animosity between this Delaware /Lumbee Indian woman and her Scots-Irish daughter-in-law. My mother and I are named for Louisa—Louise is our middle name. Healdton, Oklahoma, ca. 1925.

Page 25: "The Etymology of Honky Tonk." My family has always loved to go honky tonkin'. From the left, my great-aunt Rosalie Sanderson and her husband Lester, family friends Wilda and Cecil, Luther and Jeanette Sanderson (my grandparents), Parley Sanderson and his wife Chris(tine), my great-grandparents, Henry and Iness (Exendine) Sanderson (parents of all the other Sandersons in the photo), Lillie Mae Sanderson and her husband Orlie and Enna

Sanderson and her husband Billy. (Spouses' and friends' family names suppressed to protect the innocent.) We have at least three more honky tonk photos in our family collection, including one with my grandmother's mother in attendance. Taken at Sky View Club, Duncan, Oklahoma, ca. 1951.

Page 26: "Body Snatcher." My mother and brother in their Nomex® and hardhats. They were both working for Dowell Services, my mother as a mud engineer—nationally, one of two women mud engineers in the field at the time. Seminole, Oklahoma, 1979.

Page 31: "For My Brother." My brother Phillip proudly showing off his new big rig. Odessa, Texas, 1996.

Page 36: "My Great Great Grandmother Writes the Perfect Poem." My great-great-grandmother Mary Ellen Mathis Rodgers Trepanier. Tonopah, Nevada, ca. 1938.

Page 39: "My Sister's Sacrifice." My sister, Nancy Ellen, in her Hardee's uniform. Seminole, Oklahoma, 1982.

Page 41: "Work Is Love Made Visible." My Granny, Mary Jeanette Roberts Sanderson, at home with more work to do. Chickasha, Oklahoma, ca. 1940.

Page 43: My great-aunt Lavinia Pauline (Polly) Roberts Cook. She worked at the Douglass Aircraft plant in Santa Monica during WWII.

Page 45: "A Woman's Inheritance." We don't know this woman's name (holding the baby), but we think she belongs to my great-grandpa's family (Sanderson, Exendine, Farr).

Page 48: "Lessons from Luke." My grandpa Luther Leland "Luke" Sanderson at one of his many jobs, pump jockey and mechanic. The license plate says it's 1937, so he would have been twenty-two. Healdton, Oklahoma.

About the Author

Jeanetta Calhoun Mish is a native Oklahoman who returned home after twenty years to study for her PhD in American Literature and to grow good tomatoes. She lives in Norman, Oklahoma, with her husband, an engineering professor; they have a combined family of three sons, all between the ages of 17 and 19. Her mother and grandmother live just down the road.

She has participated in poetry readings and workshops for more than 20 years, including repeat performances as a founding member of the Woody Guthrie Poets at the Woody Guthrie Free Folk Festival in Okemah, Oklahoma. Other venues include Telluride Institute's Native American Writers Program; The Taos Poetry Circus Invitational Reading; Red Dirt Book Festival; Scissortail Creative Writing Festival; C.W. Post Poetry Center at LIU; Readings Against the End of the World and New York State Writers Institute Community Voices Series, both in Albany, NY; and The Knitting Factory in New York City.

Jeanetta's first collection of poetry, *Tongue Tied Woman*, won the Edda Poetry Chapbook Competition for Women in 2002. She has published recently in *LABOR: Studies in Working Class History of the Americas* and in *Oklahoma Today*. Her essay, "This Oklahoma We Call Home," appears in the Fall/Winter 2008 issue of *Crosstimbers*.

For more information, visit www.tonguetiedwoman.com.